The Forgotten
Corner of the
Garden

DIANE M. REAVES

authorHOUSE®

AuthorHouse™
1663 Liberty Drive
Bloomington, IN 47403
www.authorhouse.com
Phone: 1 (800) 839-8640

Published by AuthorHouse   01/10/2018

ISBN: 978-1-5462-2347-4 (sc)
ISBN: 978-1-5462-2346-7 (e)

You may think survivors of horrific child abuse have no reason to complain, let alone attempt to write books to share their experiences. But I think it's important for others to know what such a life is like. Living under the control of others. The pain of others. The neglect of others.

I have always been honest with all my experiences. But you need to remember this; It was *not my choice* to be abused. It was not my choice to endure, not only physical abuse, but emotional and psychological abuse. It was not my choice to endure sexual abuse.

Some may say, "why didn't you run away, or report it?"

I did both, and many, many times. I was dragged back every single time I ran away! Every single time I told someone about what was going on, it mattered not. I was *still* returned to the den of Hell. But it didn't matter. I told the Police in absolute terror what was going on. I begged them in hysterical tears, and vomiting, what was going on. And they still forced me to go back there!

This left some scars as well. Crying out for help and being totally ignored and returned to the scene of horrific abuse.

I wanted to share some *statistics* on the state of child abuse in the United States.

Did you know, every single year, 3.6 *million* referrals are made to the Child Protective Services Offices?

In the United States, 4 to 7 children, *a day*, DIE from child abuse and child neglect.

A report of child abuse is made *every 10 seconds.*

3.2 million kids EACH YEAR have been subjected to a CPS investigation.

The United States has one of the worse records in child abuse cases.

In 2014, *702,000* of child abuse were found. This would pack *(10)* modern football stadiums!

Children who have endured (6) or more abuse experiences, have an average life expectancy of *two decades shorter!*

Health issues associated with Child Abuse are:

1). Ischemic Heart Disease
2). Chronic Obstructive Pulmonary Disease
3). Liver Disease

Mental Health Disorders, Addictions and Related Problems:

1). Risk for Intimate partner violence
2). Alcoholism & Alcohol Abuse
3). Illicit drug abuse
4). Smoking and drinking at an early age
5). Depression
6). Suicide *Attempts* (plural)

Financial Impact of Child Abuse:

Lifetime estimates of lost worker productivity, health care costs, special education costs, child welfare expenditures and criminal justice expenditures are upwards of a staggering *$124 BILLION* – and this is from 2008.

This could send *1.7 Million* children to college.

In 2014, and estimated *1,580* children DIED from abuse or neglect A DAY!!!

1,580 children x 365 days a year come to = *576,700* deaths a YEAR!

80% of these deaths involve at least one parent of the child.

14% of all men in prison, and *36% of all women* in prison, in the United States were abused as a child.

An abused child is *9 times* more likely to become involved in criminal activity.

And bear in mind, please, that some of these numbers are *low ball estimates.*

So if you still think, being a survivor of horrific abuse means your life is just like any other kids, you might want to do me a favor and rethink that.

I'm here to share that not enough was done, when I needed help. And certainly not enough is being done today. And instead of the President of the USA deciding to call Opiates a Health Emergency – He needs to study these numbers and talk to people like me.

I didn't decide to take drugs to become addicted – that was some people's *choice!*

I didn't decide to stick a needle filled with heroin in my arm either. I'm sorry about those who lost loved ones to this addiction. But forgive me for feeling angry and bitter because I deserved to get this same kind of help and attention that they are receiving!

It was not my damn choice to be abused! It was not my choice to be raped! It was not my choice to endure decades, hell, a life time, of the effects of what that abuse has done to me. It wasn't my choice to decide that abusers and tormentors were to be protected with a Statute of Limitations on their crimes. While the victim has to suffer the effects for the rest of their lives!

And if you happen to be a parent, who has taken years to ensure your children do not suffer the fate you were forced to swallow – you deserve a lot of credit! It makes my stomach churn when I'm told I was "over protective" or I "over indulged" - Hell yeah I was, and did! What else would you expect based on what I had to endure?!

As I have told my husband of 32 years repeatedly, "I have no idea how to be a good parent. I have no idea how to be a good mom. All I am doing is winging it. All I want is for my children to have a childhood. I didn't. I want my children to know the love and kindness of a mom. I didn't. I want them to believe they are beautiful and strong. Build them up with confidence and courage. Because I had none of those things."

I tried to be the kind of mom that I always wanted. But I still believe it just wasn't enough.

I hate what I've had to endure. I hate my childhood. I hate what my mother, who was supposed to protect me, did to me. I hate that nobody in the family stopped her. I hate that my father didn't protect and save me. I have hated myself for so many years because of what she has done to me. Hated looking in the mirror because I see an ugly little girl. Yes, little girl. I am still stuck in that period of her wretched words and evil acts against me.

And if anyone dares to tell you it's easy, or forget about the past and move on. Kindly slap their face off! It wasn't easy! And you cannot forget a part of your life that has shaped the over protective person that you have been molded into.

And if you happen to figure out how to do so, well, let me in on it.

I was raised to be insecure. I was raised to hate myself. I was raised to believe my mother had the power to actually read my mind. My thoughts were not even safe! I was raised on just enough, and barely that, food to survive. I was tormented and abused. Beaten down physically and mentally. I believed when she told me I was ugly. I believed when she told me I was stupid. I believed when she said I was fat. I believed I wasn't entitled to anyone's love or kindness.

And I still work on changing my train of thought, to this very day.

So please don't try to tell me I need to get over it and move on. Her abuse has been carved into my flesh!! And I have the scars to prove it!

I wish all my children could look at me and say, "I had an amazing mom. She tried and sacrificed everything she had, and knew, just to make sure I wasn't harmed in any way, by anybody. I am proud of her strength. I am proud of her faith. No one could have loved me more than my mom. And I respect her for what she has suffered and still able to love."

"Nothing is more beautiful than a real smile
that has struggled through tears."

FAITH

I was born in a small cape cod style house in Milford, Connecticut on Wepawaug Drive.

My father left me and my siblings behind to separate from our mother, when I was ten years old. That day is forever carved into my memory. He announced to us, with suitcases in tow, that he was leaving. No explanation or apologies. I remember, well, the fear that suddenly swallowed me whole.

I began to cry very quietly. Then ran over to him and tried to take his suitcases out of his hand. He was talking, but I heard nothing. He opened the front door and began to walk out.

I grabbed the bottom of his tan overcoat. I held on to that damn coat as tightly as my little hands could. He, literally, had to peel my fingers off of his coat and pushed me to the ground. While yelling at me to, "just stop it!"

I fell back on the floor and watched, as I wept, while he climbed into his blue T-Bird and drove away.

I had no idea, at that age of ten, that he had another family in Brooklyn. A woman named Lenore Belzer and her two daughters, Francine and Debra.

I hated him for leaving.

His leaving affected my entire life. He left to enjoy a new life void of me and my siblings. I hated him for not protecting us. He *knew* what our mother was doing to us. Yet he still turned his back, on that day, and walked away.

My mother hated him for leaving as well. And we had to pay the price for her hatred and anger. A price we dearly paid.

My personal faith was beyond tested. I was to endure horrific physical, mental, emotional and sexual abuse for seven more long, hard years. At seventeen, I was removed from this den of Hell. But not by my father.

I didn't have a relationship with my father for years. I was very angry. I cried out to God to save me or let me die. I begged my dad to save me. Neither one answered me.

After being kidnapped and given a different name, so that our father wouldn't find us. I had an opportunity to get away from my mother.

I suffered hysterical blindness, as well as, severe panic attacks and was diagnosed with PTSD.

Many years crawled by as I ventured into changing my life as a *victim* of abuse, to a *survivor.*

I eventually began a relationship with my father. Yet, there was always the veil of resentment of his abandoning me. But I tried.

I took his leaving quite personally. I felt perhaps I was too ugly, like my mother drilled into my head. Perhaps I was too stupid, as she raised me to believe. Perhaps I just wasn't the kind of daughter he even wanted.

I would never be a daddy' girl that was certain.

At the age of thirty, I was married but had no children. I was told by many expensive doctors that I was unable to conceive. Due to extreme physical trauma. So this, I had accepted.

I thought perhaps it's a good thing because what if I turned out to be just like her?!

One night, my dad called. He told me how proud of me he was and that he loved me. My dad *never* told me that before in my entire thirty years of existence. But it made my night. I was actually very happy.

Four days later, in the early morning hours, my phone rang. Hubby answered it and quickly handed the phone to me. My sister in law was on the other end. She was crying. I sat up and turned the light on. She told me, between tears, that my father was dead. My first thought was he must have had a heart attack because he was a heavy smoker.

"No," she said. It wasn't a heart attack. He killed himself.

My mind couldn't grasp what she was saying. Suicide? No, way!

"Yes, Diane. Your brother and I just found him. He still had the shot gun wedged between his knees.

Apparently, he had taken his life *four* days earlier. The very night he had

called me to say how proud he was of me, and that he loved me.

He left a two-page note behind.

At his funeral, when everyone had left, I stayed behind alone. I waited at his grave side until they lowered him into the dark earth. I fell to my knees and wept. I knew it would be the last time I would ever see him again, this side of Heaven.

At the age of ten years old, my dad left me in the hands of a living monster. And here I was at the age of thirty and my dad was leaving me all over again.

Exactly four months later, *to the day*, I was told that I was pregnant. I refused to believe the doctor until she grabbed me by the hand and took me into the ultra sound room where she showed me proof that I was with child.

How I cried the day my daughter Jenny was born. Cried because I wanted my father to be there. But I guess he never was really there at all.

Every single year, at Christmas, I get to remember my dad blowing his brains out. And every Christmas since our three children have been born, they have had to witness their mom's broken heart, and anguish, remembering the day their grandfather left me again.

If he were alive today, he wouldn't recognize me. And that's a good thing.

I've yet to visit his grave. I've never seen his grave stone. It's something I have been unable to do.

The impact my dad's life, and death, has had on me is profound. Soon after, my mother took her life as well.

It was the first time, in my entire life, that I actually felt safe.

"He that has no charity deserves no mercy." Author Unknown

UNLIMITED MERCIES

How I pray for God's mercy upon us. But, at times, I truly don't believe we deserve it.

If I have failed, my Lord, I am truly sorry and pray You will continue to work in me. If I have failed my children, I pray He will continue to work in each of them. I honestly did, and do, the best I am capable of. No one is perfect, yet we are to strive for perfection.

If I knew then, what I know now, I know my life would be completely different. This just tells me it was not the will of God for me to have that knowledge. Because He, too, knows it would have changed my path.

As it is, I have found that I am a remnant of His chosen people. What an awesome miracle is that? Thank our Father for all we endure, because we don't know the mind of Almighty God.

He knew us before we were born. I imagine having conversations with Him, and them going something like this, "Send me to the worse parents, Lord! Let me be filled with horrors and nightmares. Let me see the dark spirits that dwell upon the earth. Let me be beaten, burned, poisoned, raped, and mentally screwed. Let me endure my own earthly father's suicide. Let me be so broken I attempt it myself. Because *even* if I should endure all of these things, and *so much more*, I will never stop loving You, Lord God."

I'm pretty sure that's not really how it went. But a girl can dream.

We all have to fight the demons who reign here. Fight the fears we carry within. Fight our strong wills of survival that often prevent us from *letting go and letting God.*

I do not share my story to garner any sympathy or pity. I want neither. I share my story because we all have a story. We are all here for His will. We all have a mission. Perhaps we just haven't figured it out yet.

Love with all your might. Pray without ceasing. Forgive the unforgivable. Give your best when others are in need. Beg for the comfort and peace that God has. Remember how much God loves each and every one of us.

One day, when I walk with Him in His glorious Kingdom, none of this life will even matter. He will take away all the pain, the tears and the loss. I will be filled with a new Spirit and will cease to remember the Hell I have endured.

Our lives are short. I need to remember my mission. If only I had the ability to enable *all* people to see and feel the love of our Lord. How much happier we would all be. For all to learn forgiveness and generosity. For all to share so no one has to do without. It would be Heaven on earth. But I'm afraid God is not ready for that yet. I wish all would change so that they would not have to experience His wrath. Or to face an eternity without His Light or presence.

Pray without ceasing. Love without boundaries. Pray for your families. Pray for our leaders. Pray for our world. Pray for our friends. And pray for ourselves.

"I wish Heaven had visiting hours." Author Unknown

YESTERDAY

I cannot believe it is just shy of 28 years since my father took his life, because for me, it was yesterday.

February marks the loss of my baby brother Teddy. Who brought me closer to God. He died after enduring a living Hell called leukemia. How he suffered.

October marks the loss of my older sister Sharon who was born with Downs Syndrome. But had a heart of pure gold, straight from Heaven. When I dream of Sharon, she is utterly happy. Her smile and laughter stay with me. She died of a brain aneurysm.

November marks the loss of my other baby brother Adam. He died of a sudden double heart attack. He suffered from liver complications for years.

How my heart is bursting with grief and sadness. How I miss each one so desperately. I have cried an ocean. And often wonder how we are expected to deal with such loss. But then remember we really have no other choice do we?

"The company of many doesn't erase
the loss of one." Unknown

ILLUSION

Was I ever beautiful in my youth, or was it just a hopeful illusion? So many colors of countless seasons that have washed over me. If only we could stand above our world and see below what is to come.

For the peace and joy of youth changes with the years. We desperately try to hold tight to the rays of sun, only to watch as they turn to shadows.

Was I ever truly worthy enough to be found by the wealth of love? For it feels as though I have been found to be bankrupt of such a privilege.

To hide from another sunrise after being witness to so many, for fear the colors will begin to fade.

I have lost interest in the disappearing of hours and cling to timelessness.

Have I done all I have been sent to accomplish? Will I know when the final task has been completed?

Will God reach down His might hand and scoop me to Him?

To feel the breath of Father for all eternity.

To love so dearly, and be denied such in return, is a punishment no one deserves.

For can the early morning dew mend the cracks within our very soul? Or the rain wash us clean from our transgressions?

Was I ever beautiful enough, or smart enough, to be desired of one who could give anyone the world?

Or has all of this existence merely been a dream I have yet to wake from. A dream I have created myself because my reality was too harsh to bear.

Where has it all gone? Have I over stayed my welcome? Will my final day be easier than my entire voyage?

"Everything has beauty, but not everyone sees it." Unknown

SPIRIT KILLER

I wonder who it was that my mother killed in me when I was so very young.

Who was I?

Did I even have a chance at *being* before her?

What would I have been like if *she* had not been?

No doll babies, no coloring books, no cartoons, no Christmas gifts, no pretty dresses or shoes. No hair bows or jewelry. No pretty coats and hats. No pretty bed or bedroom.

What kind of girl would I have been if she hadn't killed me?

What fears would have been gone if she had not planted, and nurtured, them?

What nightmares would have never been dreamt if she had not forced me to live them?

How differently would I have been in academics and socially?

What did she see when she looked at me? What was it that she had to kill?

How many times did she feel it necessary to break me?

Who was I before *she* was?

"God takes hold of the heart and when the heart is taken *all* is won!" Matthew Henry

MY PERSONAL TESTIMONY
AT CHURCH

When I look back on my childhood, and unfortunately I do, I am always amazed that I actually survived it. For it was wrought with a kind of misery and torment that you wouldn't wish upon anyone. After all, a happy childhood is not worth sharing, is it?

I've heard so many complain about how terrible their early years were, but they didn't have to survive Connie, my mother.

By the grace of Almighty God, I am saved. I believe it was that same grace that saved me from my childhood. There were no hugs and kisses. Never heard the words, "I love you," uttered. No pretty lace dresses. No baby dolls to play with. No books to read. There was no ice cream Sundays or pancake breakfasts. No warm clothes or even a radio to listen to. I grew up without the luxury of a sheet and pillow, or warm toasty blanket.

I slept in a bare room with only an iron bed in it. An iron bed I was tied to at night. As I would hear my mother walk out and lock the door behind her, I was left there. Lying in darkness. Freezing cold in the winter and dying from heat stroke in the summer. It was a good day *if* the boards were removed from the windows.

I used to love to listen to the birds singing away outside. I could hear all the neighborhood kids playing, screaming with laughter. Riding their bikes up and down Wepawaug Drive. I used to get this anxious feeling when I would hear the ice cream truck's bell coming down the street. Oh, how I wanted to be there, standing on the curb with a quarter, waiting for an ice cream cone.

I was always so hungry, thirsty too. Connie's excuse for *not* feeding me was because I was a very bad little girl. And very bad little girls didn't deserve to eat or drink. Or, apparently, use the bathroom either. But I *did* deserve to be beaten with fists or objects. I *did* deserve to life threatening injuries while attempting to run away from Connie. Like when I ran right through a plate glass door, which nearly severed my right arm.

I *did* deserve to be burned and kept in a cage like an animal. Funny thing, I can't ever remember our dog Dukie ever being kept in a cage. I *did* deserve to have my front teeth knocked right out of my head. Being a bad little girl also entitled me to emotional abuse, mind games, being subject to Black Magic. After all, Connie did make an actual pact with the devil. And she had me believing that she could even read my mind. To me, not even my own thoughts were safe.

On special days, Connie would force a bar of soap down my throat. Delivered in the most brutal, vial way possible. She would throw me down on the floor, face up. Naturally, I would try to keep my mouth completely closed. Such horrific fear I felt. My mother knew I was not going to open my mouth willingly, no matter how much she threatened me. So she would then plug my nose. I held on as long as I could without the ability to breathe. But eventually, I had to open my mouth to get air. And that's when she would thrust that damn bar of soap in my mouth with such a force I thought she would break my teeth! I had to pay, after all, for not allowing her to do it without plugging my nose.

She would take that bar and grind it over and over and over in my mouth. She would grind it in all my teeth. So much would go down my throat because I was laying on my back. When she was done with her brutal attack. She would climb off of me and I would run as fast as my feet would carry me, out back door in the kitchen. Where I would race to the yard and fall to my knees and violently vomit for hours. It was beyond vicious. I have permanent damage to my stomach because of all the soap and bleach I have been forced to ingest. Connie loved to add bleach or Comet to food we were fed.

And heaven help you when it was time for a bath. No Mr. Bubble for me. Connie's preference was steel wool pads and cleanser. Scrubbing your skin raw! On holidays, like Christmas, instead of gifts, I was lucky enough to receive a stocking filled with black stones. And told, "that's what bad girls get!"

I lived in absolute terror of Connie. She was cruel beyond measure. I have scars on the outside of my body, but honestly, the ones on the *inside* are the hardest to heal.

She kidnapped us and changed our names. And we were forced to live in some pretty horrific places, including a tent. Skipping all over the country, living like gypsies.

I ran away, and ran away. I would hide places I thought she would never find me. But she always did. She kept having me arrested. She would have me charged with being *incorrigible*-ME, incorrigible!! At that time, I didn't even know what the word meant.

I have cut my wrists. Taken over 100 pills and over dosed. Stood on the George Washington Bridge, in the dead of winter, and attempted to jump.

I felt *death* was far better than what I was living. But God had a plan for me. God saw my future even when I could not.

So many times I fell to my knees, sick and vomiting. My head exploding. My stomach on fire. Heaving the poison I had ingested which was fed to me. Just weeping. Crying out to God. "Why God? Why do I have to suffer like this? Why does she hate me? What have I done to deserve this? Please tell me. Please forgive me!" I felt I was being punished. Not only by Connie for being such a "bad little girl," but also by God. I felt my words of anguish always fell on deaf ears. Nobody was listening.

I suffered for *years* under Connie's rule. Under her cruelties. Her torture. Her abuse. Locks on the doors. Locks on the cupboards. Locks on the phone. Locks on the refrigerator. Where was my Knight in shining armor? Where was my guardian angel? I used to believe because my mother hated me, God must hate me as well. What mother can hate her own daughter?

I have suffered from hysterical blindness. Anorexia. Severe panic attacks. Depression. Horrific nightmares and have been diagnosed with PTSD. And if this wasn't enough, my dad decided to load a shot gun, wedge it between his knees. Stick it in his mouth and pull the trigger. He did so right before Christmas. So there will *never* be a Christmas, for the rest of my life, that would pass without this gruesome reminder of self murder. And certainly not to be outdone by his act of shear violence, Connie decided to take her life as well.

How much is too much?

When Connie died, I wept for four days straight. I cried because it was the first time, in my *entire* life, that I actually felt safe. Do you know what that feels like?

My children had never met her, but they know some of what I have endured because of her. I have worked very hard to get some semblance of a life. I have worked very hard to ensure that the cycle of abuse *ended with me.*

Could I have ever survived any of these horrors, and so much more, that I have not shared here without God in my life?

No! I could not have. If God did not dwell within my heart and soul, I could be a prostitute, a drug addict, a drunk, a child abuser. Or even a daughter who murdered her own abusive mother. Our prisons are filled with such.

God *never* said it would be *easy.* He never said we would not suffer. But He did promise *to be with us.* Even if, at times, we don't think He is. Trust me, He is with you.

If not for the strength and courage of God in my life, I would not be here before you. I *need* God in my daily life. I need God to hold my hand when I wake up unable to breathe and petrified. Weeping uncontrollably because I've had yet another horrific nightmare about Connie tormenting me.

I need to envision what my life, my eternal life, will be like in the company of Angels and Prophets. While walking side by side with our Lord and Savior, Jesus Christ.

And I will attempt to learn as much as I can about the teachings of our Lord. Learn as much as I can about *attempting* to reach perfection. If I endeavor to live by the characteristics of Christ, and try to share with others the amazing, healing, forgiving, merciful, tough love that our Father has for every single one of us. How our Savior would have died on that cross *even if* it meant His act would have saved only ONE person!

He forgives our sins. We *have* to forgive others their sins as well. I am not my mother's judge. I want nothing to do with her judgment.

God teaches us to love our enemies. But what if your enemy, your tormentor, your abuser is your own mother?

I'm afraid there are no loop holes. Jesus taught we must love our enemies. "Whoever loves God must also love his brother."

To me, it's been actually more difficult to *forget* than it has been to *forgive.*

Though the horrific memories are etched upon my soul, I will strive to engrave upon my heart the words and lessons of our heavenly Father all the rest of my days. As many days as Father allows me to enjoy.

"How great is the love the Father has lavished on us, that we should be called Children of God! And that is what we are!"

We serve an awesome God. And this testimony truly glorifies Him and all He is capable of. He is the Deliverer. Taking us from bondage to freedom.

Eleanor Roosevelt said, "God takes man into deep water; not to drown him but to cleanse him."

"Sometimes I just look up, smile and say,
"I know that was you." Unknown

BROTHERLY FEED BACK

The following is a letter from my brother Adam. We were supposed to be writing this second book of mine together. He was called home shortly after we had decided to do so.

These are my brother's own words to me.

"I read your book, Diane. I found it to be very interesting. I wish you had told me you had written one. I just happened to come across it while searching on Amazon.

There were a few surprises, but mostly things I obviously already knew.

The chapter about Teddy made me cry.

I find it fascinating how two people, living in the same house, at the same time, can take away different memories.

I think that mostly comes from the fact that when you finally escaped, you still couldn't break free for so long. I had trouble breaking free, but it happened at a much younger age for me.

And I didn't experience anything close to the brutal, physical and psychological abuse that you suffered, Diane.

There was abuse for me as well, but it was more of a mind fuck than anything else. Reading some of the chapters brought back so many horrible memories I had buried.

It made me remember how mom would wrap your hair around her fist and drag you kicking and screaming down the hallway into the bathroom. Where she would force feed you so much soap you would come charging out of that bathroom. Run outside where you would vomit for, what seemed, hours on end. How she didn't kill you, Diane, I don't know.

Your chapter on Teddy made me cry because I felt the same way about him. I was there in the standing room only, with even more people outside watching monitors to pay their respect.

I listened to the *thirteen* eulogies. Listened to the choir sing at his grave site as the Pastor cried.

Teddy was a great man of God. And he has made an impact in the world around him. As well as, in eternity.

Our mother knew all of our insecurities and she preyed on them. Her particular game with me was telling me that I would never amount to anything. Like how she drilled into your head that you were ugly, fat and stupid. You were none of those things, Diane. She knew what to say to hurt us the most.

She told me that I would never do anything of value and that I would die old and alone because I would never find a woman foolish enough to love me. Or foolish enough to have my children.

She tried to teach me that nothing at all endures the test of time and all is doomed to failure.

Mom knew that fear of impending doom was a far more effective weapon then brutality. As her sinister nature matured, she learned that abusing the mind was far more effective than the way she abused your body.

It is much easier to *control* someone paralyzed from fear of the world around them, then controlling someone paralyzed by fear of her.

God prevails for those that seek Him.

I am a flawed man. But I have received blessings far beyond my wildest dreams. I nourish those blessings and I thank God for His mercy and kindness every single day.

Diane, to your children I say, You don't have to say any more than thank you to Almighty God, for blessing you all with a mother that would rather *die* for you instead of hurt you, as she was hurt.

Jenny, Andrew and Mary, you all need to say thanks for the blessing you have in your mom. You need to hold her close because she *deserves* as much love as she gives.

If your mom wasn't who she is today, *you* wouldn't be who you are today. I don't think anyone that knows you, even a little, wouldn't want you to be who you all are today.

For you all bring joy and innocence. And a bit of silliness to those around you. That is *just as much* a product of *your mom's suffering* than anything else!

Your mom asks, several times in her book, "why?" Maybe the answer lies in the legacy that she leaves the world; her three children.

For I truly believe that the only legacy one leaves on the world has nothing to do with wealth and fame.

It's our children.

Diane, I was moved, and I was so touched. And I am jealous. *I* wanted to write the book first.

I love you,

Adam

"I hope I'll see you on the other side of the stars." Unknown

I HATE CHRISTMAS

Twenty-eight Christmas' have come and gone since my dad left us.

I pray he is in heaven and has found true peace for his tormented soul.

I will not claim to know what was in his mind when he pulled that trigger. But I have to believe he was at his wits end and felt he had no other choice.

Depression and anxiety are, most often, silent killers among us. Dealing with either is difficult. When some see utter darkness, and cannot envision the light, it leads to brokenness.

When a loved one takes their own life, it may end *their* pain and sorrow. But it leaves that pain as their destiny. And it brings many a mighty man, and woman, to their knees.

Merry Christmas to my dad who is missed terribly and has created such a severe ache within my heart and soul that never diminishes.

32

"There are no shortcuts to any place worth going." Helen Keller

HISTORICAL PREVENTION

If you know me, you know what I have been forced to endure.

You will also know what measures I had to take in order to maintain my sanity.

To say it was a hard, long, painful road, would be a serious under statement. For it was so much more.

As a mom, it is my entire life's work to protect my children.

As an adult, it is my job to ensure the futures of my children are *better* than mine was. It was my sole responsibility to do the right thing by each of them. In my attempts, and estimations, I have done the best I was capable of doing.

For the cycle *of abuse has not* been repeated. My actions were my own and not what I was taught by others cruelties.

The horrors were *not* ever visited on mine. Even though those cruelties lived in me. We may be able to tame the memories, but we will *never* kill them.

One of the hardest pills I've had to swallow was when one of my own children told me how *unfair* it was to *them* that they had me as their mom. Unfair to have to *deal* with seeing me endure severe panic attacks.

Unfair to have to wake me from having another horrific nightmare and having to convince me that I was *safe*, as I wept uncontrollably.

Not showing *an ounce* of sympathy for all I was *forced* to endure. All I had no choice about. Yet, instead of becoming what I had survived, and just barely at that, I worked my tail off to ensure my children would be safe and protected. And if necessary, even from me.

I would rather die than ever put them through the Hell I survived.

I did my job. And never looked for any rewards for doing what *moms are supposed to do.*

One day, when I am gone, I just hope and pray my children realize how much I did for them so that their lives, and futures, would be incredible.

They were able to have a childhood, and so much more. They were able to have all that I never had. And all that I ever wanted. Just seems, at times, that it still isn't enough for them.

Because when they have children of their own, they certainly won't have to do all that I have had to do. And what a blessing that is.

"Be sure you put your feet in the right place. Then stand firm!" Abe Lincoln

THE HEM OF YOUR CLOAK

If there are lessons to be learned by our personal sufferings, these lessons can easily be lost because of despair.

How difficult it is to have to endure so much misery, day by day. Literally hour by hours and somehow find a lesson in the mire of great depression and weakness.

When strength is gone. When courage is lost. When knees are raw, what pray tell, then?

Feeling abandoned by everyone in our path and feeling even the Lord has left our side, is too great to bear.

Pleading for His tender mercies. But feeling absolutely exhausted.

What value does a life have when filled with such overwhelming effort to merely make it through another hours?! Where is the purpose of such? What is the Father silent, and unyielding, to the cries of His beloved Saints?

Oceans of tears, endless prayers. Knocking, banging, storming the door to His very heart. Attempting so desperately to incline His ear.

Our forefather saw signs and wonders. We would be satisfied with a mere touch of His hem to heal the daily agony of living.

"Forget what hurt you, but never forget what it taught you." Unknown

LINEAGE

How is it possible to feel nostalgic for a homeland you have never been to?

Questions that are refused, let alone ever answered.

Secrets, well hidden, for so long that it takes clues from Heaven above to reveal them one by one.

Feeling a pull towards a place never seen. Yet feeling a part of you has been there. Grown there. Lived there. And died there.

Ghettos of absolute desperation. Bare essentials in food and drink. Locked away, fenced off. Spit at, kicked down, turned over to tormentors. Robbed of all you have held so dear. Generations of memories and treasures gone.

All ripped from your grasp. Forced to sit in silence and watch as parts of your very existence are robbed.

Watching as loved ones are torn from each others embrace. Children dragged off weeping. Mothers and fathers separated into crowded, dark and cold train cars.

Winter's bite never felt quite so harsh and unrelenting before.

The homes no longer look the same. Crowded all together as cattle in iron pens.

Warmth no longer exists from within. There are no longer clouds of fresh baked Sabbath bread escaping from windows.

Sickness and disease grab hold of so many who have already been beaten down. What do they dream of under these frozen roofs and shared wooden bunk structures? Are they even able to sleep at all?

For so many years I have felt something was horribly wrong. I felt all the whispers and strong language spoken meant something dark. Nobody ever shared the truth.

Years passed and my research continued. As technology raced to catch up with me, the day finally came when testing could be done on my own DNA.

Finding relatives I was told all my life were dead. Finding extended family that popped up who shared the same DNA. But the most frightening information that came was the discovery of my own Jewish lineage.

And names of many death camps which had taken more relatives than I thought imaginable.

My ancestors who fled, and survived, changed their names. They even changed their religion.

A history so far away that had been held a secret for more than half my life, was finally unfolding before my eyes.

How is it that I was the one who had the unrelenting urge to hunt for the truth? And even when I found it, some refused to even accept it.

Some say to me that I am *not* a real Jew because to believe in Jesus Christ means you're not Jewish.

I had no choice.

It was taken from me. And I know full well how different my entire life would have been if I were raised as an Orthodox Jewish young woman.

In order to even be considered a Jew by strict guidelines, I have to convert and *deny* Jesus Christ. They do not believe in the whole Messianic Jewish movement. But I beg to differ, as I usually do. My heritage was stolen from me. My background was a complete fabrication. My traditions were lost. My bloodline was fictitious. And even when I asked, in writing, for information when my search had just begun, I was told, "it's none of your business." The only thing *that* did was fuel my drive to find out the truth. Made quite clear to me that something was being hidden.

I may have all the facts and truth now, and have shared them with my own children, but I still ache to go to the land of my people. I ache to see the memorial walls and buildings. The endless walls covered in photographs of the murdered. The mountains of shoes taken off their feet. To walk where so much torment was visited upon countless souls.

We think we can control so much. We think we can hide the truth. We think we can take it all to the grave with us. But we can't. And there is *nothing* that will ever be hidden from Almighty God.

"You put your arms around me and I'm home." Unknown

8,030 MOONS

How many moons have come and gone? How many footsteps have I walked, paced, when you were ill and all I could do was walk thru it?

How many hours have I prayed. Worried about what you were doing and if you were okay? How many sleepless nights have I had. Just waiting for you to fall into dreamland? Then watch as you lay there sleeping in silence?

How many times have I held you, cradled you, sang to you, fed you, bathed you, sat up with you, cried over you, prayed for and with you. Protected you, fought for you and missed you?

How many times have I told you that I love you?

With my three children, the number of moments are endless.

Since my eldest was born, I have looked into the sky and watched 8,030 moons go by. When our little ones become big ones, and no longer need us to gaze over them, to cradle them, teach them, and make them well.

We are left to look upon the countless photos of 8,030 moons gone by.

Suddenly our days become *ours* again. Our nights grow quiet again. The moments turn into hours, and the hours drag into days.

And it seems the only thing we can hope for, is an occasional call, or visit, from the ones we gave our *all* to.

Unconditionally
Unlimited
Unending

Our all is no longer needed.

How hard it was in all my attempts to be the best parent I could be. And how much I miss the little ones who *used* to need me.

"Silence is the most powerful scream." Unknown

CIRCLES

The leaves how they hang, slowly falling like a shower of golden raindrops.

Soon the air will be too cold for a single leaf to hang on to the branch it has come to call home.

As the ice dangles from the now bare branches, it dances and glistens in the sunlight.

A white blanket of snow covers the dead ground beneath it. Giving a new clean appearance to the endless hills of frozen earth.

Snuggled in it's crafted nest, a bright red cardinal, and his mate, enjoy the fruits of their labor. They now are able to dwell within.

In the distance the sound of crunching snow and ice beneath the feet of a family of deer scouting for a meal.

The long, frigid nights and short cold days seem to linger when the desire sets in to see the blooming hyacinth and daffodils.

It is a time of respite for the earth when it becomes dormant and still.

A time of great reflection of gardens past, of fruits and veggies lovingly preserved. Of those who have gone on to wait for our arrival in a better realm.

A time to draw close to warm fires and home baked treats.

A time of closeness, while patiently waiting for the warmth of the Spring sky to arrive. And return to us the new leaves that will now hang on their branches and offer to us shade beneath their cover.

"You are made higher to me and holier
because of your suffering."

Unknown

DAMAGED

If only I could have heard these words instead of being told I was, "damaged goods."

Guard your words for they will leave a permanent scar. You can never take back pain you deliver with your words. Especially, when they are used deliberately, and carefully chosen, to inflict as much pain as possible.

"Wrinkles mean you laughed. Grey hair means you cared and scars mean you lived." Unknown

THE PRAYER

Sing to me.
Tear the words from my heart.
Erase this blackness that weighs upon my every breath.
Lift the veil from mine eyes.
Show me again the light that I once knew.
That I once warmed to.
That I once waited upon.
For the wind has toppled my very soul.
And I cannot find steadfastness in my spine.
I have been robbed, by time, of the three reasons I woke each morn.
There are no longer new treasures given to me from small hands that
I can cherish.
I am left with nothing but hours and days.
They bleed into months and years.
I was meant to nurture. But now instead, I am dissolving into nothing
more than a memory.

"Just because my path is different doesn't mean I'm lost." Unknown

RAIN

How I weep for you.
Every tear falls like a piece of glass, that yet again, pierces my very soul.
This heaviness of great sorrow.
This cloud of agony.
As I fall to my knees and lose my very breath.
I cannot endure the flashes of memory that haunt me.
The echo of the sound of death vibrating in my flesh.
How could you go?
How could you leave me?
And by your own hand.
For you have left me changed forever.
And there is no going back.
The sky has fallen, and with it, has brought down the very heavens upon me.

"When life knocks you down, stand the
hell up and say, 'You hit like a girl!'"

ABYSS

There is an abyss – one spoken of in Holy Scriptures. The abyss spoken of when reading about Lazarus and the rich man.

An abyss between Heaven and Hell. An abyss which cannot be crossed. Not from the side of Heaven nor from the side of Hell.

Yet those on the side of the abyss located in Hell, *will see* others across the great divide. Will know that they cannot cross over. And will be made aware of Heaven in sight, yet unreachable.

In our lives, we come across some who we have been given discernment over. Some who *know* right from wrong. Evil from good. God from Satan.

Yet decide, even being given such knowledge, to take the road crowded with far too many souls. Walking down to the abyss of darkness and Hell that awaits. How we pray for none to become the enemy of God.

When we recognize these people, who may be in our own family, we must know when to decide that we can no longer continue to cross that abyss into Hell.

In our continued attempts to grab them from an eternity of darkness.

We all know the task of Satan. And he will use all our shortcomings and weaknesses against us.

We must all decide for ourselves.

Angel or Demon
Darkness or Light
Almighty God or Satan

"And I'd choose you; in a hundred lifetimes, in a hundred worlds, in any version of reality. I'd find you and I'd choose you." The Chaos of Stars

GOD'S RELENTLESS PURSUIT OF US

What does that mean?

Webster's defines relentless as:

Merciless, Severe, and Persistent.

Pretty intimidating words.

Imagine God's *relentless* pursuit of you, or me.

If we read the book of Jonah, it involves the horrific state of sin in the city of Ninevah. Because its, absolute, wickedness had come *before God*.

Let's imagine the *level* of wickedness to have reached God Almighty. To have reached the very throne of God.

During that time, the city of Ninevah was a huge city. It had many inhabitants. Along with the violence, its *evil ways* are described by Nahum as including, but not limited to, plotting against the Lord (Nahum 1:11).

As well as, cruelty and plundering in war, prostitution, witchcraft, and commercial exploitation. (Pretty much sounds like any town USA, doesn't it?)

So the great sins of Ninevah now reached the throne of God. God, in turn, reached out to Jonah. He called out, "Arise! Go!" Strong, simple command. Not one you can easily misunderstand.

But Jonah *knew* these people of Ninevah and he hated them! The last thing he felt these evil people deserved, was God's forgiveness.

Jonah fled from the Lord.

Do you honestly think you can ever flee from God? I wonder how Jonah felt he ever really had a choice in the matter. But, apparently, Jonah's mind, he did. And so he ran from the Lord. Fleeing in a boat to Tarshish.

God sent a great wind and a violent storm. Jonah went below deck and fell into a deep sleep. But he was soon awoken by the crew members who wanted to know who he was and where he had come from. (For they already knew he was running away from the Lord)

The sea remained wild until the crew took Jonah and threw him into the sea. Only then was the calm restored.

Jonah did not drown.

Instead, a great fish swallowed him and there he remained for three days and three nights. Imagine with me for a moment, the terror that Jonah must have felt. The waves crashing violently all around him, taking in water, "the seaweed wrapped around his head." (Jonah 2:5)

And then, *he sank*, "to the roots of the mountains." (Jonah 2:6) It's pretty dark down there at the roots of the mountains.

Then, suddenly, the fish spit Jonah out onto dry land.

The Lord spoke to Jonah a *second* time. God was *relentless* in His pursuit of Jonah. Only this time, Jonah obeyed God.

Upon Jonah's delivery of God's message and the reaction of the people *and* the king of Ninevah, "God had compassion and did not bring the destruction He had threatened." (Jonah 3:10) For the people repented and wore sackcloth and fasted.

This *enraged* Jonah to the point of no longer rejoicing that God had spared his life in the sea. But now, because of God's mercy towards the people of Ninevah, Jonah truly felt it was, "better for me to die than to live."
(Jonah 4:4)

As Jonah left the city to sit and, basically, sulk. He found shade and rested. There God provided a vine for Jonah which gave him comfort and brought him great happiness.

Then God sent a worm which destroyed the vine. Since the vine and the covering were now gone, shade was gone. The sun was allowed to scorch Jonah's face. He was so hot, he felt faint from the heat.

Again he proclaimed, "It would have be better for me to die." (Jonah 4:8)

God asked Jonah if he had any right to be angry about the vine. Jonah

insisted he did. Jonah replied, "I do. I am angry enough to die!" (Jonah 4:9)

What was God's reply to him?

"You did not tend it or make it grow, it sprang up overnight and died overnight. But Ninevah has more than a hundred and twenty thousand

people who cannot tell their right hand from their left hand. And many cattle as well. Should I not be concerned about that great city?" (Jonah 4:10)

Our Lord tried to teach Jonah of His mercy and compassion. And also that God has the first word and the last word. Regardless of what *we* may think, believe or feel.

God was attempting to teach Jonah that He took no pleasure in the death of the wicked. But He rather desired that they turn from their evil ways and live.

Of course, Jonah was grateful when God showed His mercies upon the Israelites. But only wanted his enemies to endure the wrath of God. God here rebukes such hardness, and proclaims His mercy.

God's pursuit of us is *relentless*.

We may try to fight Him. We may try to turn from Him. We may think He will leave us to ourselves. But He will pursue, *relentlessly*.

Pursue on, heavenly Father – Pursue on! Be blessed my friends, and don't try to out run the Lord.

"Having a soft heart in a cruel world is courage, *not* weakness." Unknown

INNER DEMONS

You're beaten into silence. You're frightened of every shadow.

You know the power of denial. The power of hunger. The taste of thirst.

You know what isolation feels like. You're intimate with loneliness.

Giving up is giving in when you are driven to the end of your own mind.

When courage has lost its home. And hope has never even arrived.

Darkness replaces any glimmer of light.

When you think you've heard all the ugly words that can be said about you. All the ugly words that are spoken to you daily. More seem to find a way into your hearing.

The crushing weight of despair that sits upon your heart. That robs you of the ability to breathe.

As your knees buckles from a pain that invades every single limb. You feel nothing anymore but absolute sorrow.

You choke on the tears that refuse to cease. You scream as loud as possible. The sound piercing your mind because no sound ever leaves your lips. The sound is trapped in your mind. A prisoner as you are a prisoner.

Death refuses you. Time stops. And all you want is for the pain to stop for one moment. One hour. One day.

Relentless torture. It grows like a weed. Nothing can kill it.

Yet, when freedom has been fought for, feverishly, violently, nobody even cares what roads it has taken to get here.

To be so selfish and careless. A treasure many seem to possess.

They know not the torment and suffering. It is meaningless to them.

They don't realize they are *safe* because of *me*. Because of my victories.

They are safe...

I thought it would mean so much more. I was so wrong. So terribly wrong.

"But this is slavery, not to speak one's thought." Euripides

DO ANGELS WEEP?

This is another hard memory for me. I lost my baby brother, Teddy, to his long battle with leukemia, Valentines Day.

I could not ask for a finer, kinder, more loving baby brother than Teddy. I was blessed beyond measure. I was honored to call him "brother." How he loved our Lord and Savior with all that he was. Spent years traveling all over the world. He helped set up churches, and brought many brothers and sisters to Christ.

He lived across the country from me, but that didn't stop us from sharing many hours on the phone. Keeping up with each others lives. He left behind a young wife and three small children. His youngest, my niece, was only five.

Teddy's leukemia was not one that was a genetic strain. His was contracted from an environmental strain. He was exposed to chemicals found in certain paints used on Boeing airplanes. The masks they provided did not protect them from the lethal doses of exposure.

My brother Teddy was the last in a group of men, who had all contracted this viral leukemia. They had all died. Teddy was the last one to pass. Of course there was a Class Action Lawsuit. The ones left behind were paid off. How horrific. How sad. For they would all have rather had no money, and their loved ones beside them.

Teddy was so strong. Honestly, I can't imagine being half as strong as he was. What he endured for years. The bruises. The breaking of his bones, time and time again. The hospital stays due to the horrific effects that the chemo had on his frail body.

He was my bear! But the chemo changed him into a twig of that bear. He had lost so much weight, all his hair, all his strength.

When his bouts at the hospital were over, usually lasting for more than a month at a time. Teddy would immediately travel again. Making sure he could help to set up one more church before he left us all behind. He loved God so very much, and yes, as we all do, he questioned why he had to endure such great pain. Such great sickness. His faith had been tested more than once.

At this time, I began having trouble with my heart. I didn't know at the time that it was merely an issue with change of life, and severe dehydration. But, when we would talk, I would tell him how scared it was for me. Feeling I was faced with death. And that I began to keep a journal for my children. I began writing letters to them and to my husband. I wanted to prepare things that I could leave behind for them to find after I was gone. Teddy loved that idea. He told me he had started doing the same thing. And even went as far to start making video tapes for the kids. I was so happy to hear this. I knew it would mean so much to them.

We surely had the worse upbringing, but we had each other. When he was a little baby, I would sing him to sleep every night. I was very young, only five years old. The only song that I knew all the words to was Silent Night. How silly to think about it now. But, I would sing that song to him over and over until he fell fast asleep. I took care of him like he was my baby.

He told me before he passed, that he always remembered me singing that silly song to him. He knew all the words to it by the time he was five. He also told me how he remembered how I taught him how to write. And how to spell long before he went to school. I was so tickled that he actually remembered all of that. I used to pretend I was a school teacher. He would sit in a chair with a little notebook and pencil. I would write words on this old chalk board with the smallest pieces of chalk. And make him write it over and over again.

My little brother baby brother. We had endured so much growing up. All he ever wanted was to meet the perfect girl and fall in love. Have lots of babies to love. I can remember how unhappy he was right before his first trip to Singapore. He was so depressed and he was very sick. I couldn't believe he was still going to make the long trip, but he did.

It was so important to him. He felt he had a mission. And he did. He sent me so many letters and post cards from every city he visited through the years. When he finally met his wife, his life changed completely. They were so in love. And I was so happy for him. He finally had all that he dreamed of.

My little baby brother. He show me so much about true happiness.

He show me so much about endurance, during the most horrible bouts of pain. The needles, the throwing up, the pain deep down inside of his very bones from all the medically needed breaks. Eventually, not even morphine worked on his pain.

He wanted so badly to have just one more year. It was always the same. Just one more year to watch my babies grow up. Just one more year to share with my wife. Just one more year to share another Christmas, another Easter, another snow storm.

Teddy suffered for nearly six long years with this illness. I don't think I would have lasted three years in such condition. He fought to be with his family. Fought to be with his wife. Fought to bring just one more person back to God.

When Teddy died, the church held close to two hundred people who came to show their last respects to my baby brother. He was so dearly loved and shared all of himself with many others.

He left a video to be shown at his own funeral service. I'm told, there wasn't a dry eye in the entire place. He had many messages for so many that he loved, including me. But when asked for same, it was never shared.

I was not there during his last breaths. I was not there when they laid him to rest beneath the earth. For I could not bring myself to watch my little baby brother Teddy leave. I could not bear that much pain.

My last words were spoken to him, through his wife, whispered in his ear as he lay in the hospital bed. She said tears rolled down his face and he smiled. But, as I type these words, I weep.

When we talked, he always understood, that when the time came, I would not be able to be there. I just couldn't. No, it's not a question of being selfish. It's a question of knowing that I would not have been able to endure it. And Teddy understood this. How truly great a love, when knowing that seeing them leave, would change our entire life.

When Teddy returned to be with God, he took a part of me with him. A part of my heart that he promised to hold until we meet again. I know he is there, waiting for me. We are going to meet under the big tree which grows beside the river of life. He will be sitting in the shade, waiting, when I go to meet him there.

I miss him terribly. I miss hearing his voice, his laughter. I miss his great big bear hugs. Nobody can ever replace them. I miss his unending kindness. I miss how even though he suffered to much, he still loved greatly.

His eyes. His smile. I miss his company. I don't much like Valentines Day anymore. It seems so many of my holidays are marked with such great loss and sadness.

To my baby brother, Teddy, I love you so much, sweet little boy. And I am Diane M. Reaves glad that you are no longer in such great pain. It ended the day Father took you to His bosom. Rest well sweet baby, I'll be there as soon as I can.

"If you fall, I'll be there." Floor

A DARK SHADOW

It is hard to fight off the emotion of hate. For everyone, there will be, or has been, times in our collectives lives that we have had the uncontrollable feelings of hate.

As a Christian, I *try* to be as forgiving as I am able. But there are many time I deeply struggle with hating the *actions* of people.

If you live a life never being cruel, or evil, towards others. When such is perpetrated upon you, it can drive us to a place of darkness.

I imagine this is the plan of Lucifer. To place such stones in our path. Stones we must step on to move forward. Stones we don't know how they even got there, but, always seem to appear under foot just when we feel the road is becoming smoother. There's just no such thing.

When others attack verbally. When others belittle us. When others hurt our children for nothing more than entertainment. When you discover others are not what they seem but are, in actuality, backstabbing liars. It's almost too much to bear.

So, naturally, the first emotion felt is a great anger. Which turns to a hatred of their *actions*. Then runs into vengeful thoughts. For we are to hate the sin and not the sinner. But how many among us make this distinction?

All at the same time feeling great sorrow and disappointment that God's creatures would actually conduct themselves this way. I incessantly drown myself in prayer.

I have had many difficult lessons in the art of forgiveness. Even when it was not asked of me. I took to heart the lesson of how so much has been forgiven of *me* by Almighty God. Therefore, I *must also* forgive.

Then I struggle with the fact that I do not do to anyone the things which have been done to me. I just wouldn't. I don't have it in me to be so utterly cruel. The degrees of sin come to mind. When one commandment is broken *all are broken*. A thief is the same as a murderer. There are no lesser sins. Sin is sin.

And yes, I also know we can never *earn* our way into His glorious Kingdom. It is only by the grace of God, and our faith in Jesus Christ. And His death as an atonement for our sins, that we may enter His gates. No amount of *good works* will earn a place for any. That also means I should still do good works. I should continue to strive for the perfection Jesus Christ lived when He walked among us.

Having to experience others sinful nature, others cruelties, others hateful actions makes my blood boil. So, yes, I want to lash out. Yes, I want to bring *them* as much pain and sorrow as they have delivered upon my doorstep.

But we are forbidden to do so.

And therein lies my struggle. Good works cannot get you into Heaven. *But bad works can get you into Hell.*

Sometimes we are lucky enough to see folks get what *we think* they deserve. And most times we will never see justice.

Please pray for me, and many others like me, who truly want to be a light unto this world of darkness. But we often struggle with the reality of such inherent weaknesses.

I cannot *physically* see our Savior. How desperately I do want to. I cannot hear His voice, as I hear others voices. But how desperately I long to. I ask Him countless questions and wish He could sit with me and tell me what to do. What to feel.

The mortal side of me wars continuously with the immortal side. The flesh against the spirit. Battle after battle.

How completely incredible it would be if what *we do* to others, *really* was done to us. But we all know that's not how it ever happens. There are more people who have died of a broken heart than you realize. For this world chews us up. Spits us out and breaks us. And when this world has done it's worst to us, we are somehow supposed to rise above that and *return love for hate.*

When we fail to see, or find, any beauty in the world because we are forced to swallow so much crap, well, I think it's no longer fruitful to even be here. Because what will ever change?

I would love for all the mean, evil, cruel, soul-less creatures to be put on an island. Away from the rest of us so that we can actually be among people who are just like we are.

Please pray for the world. It's turning into such a dark, ugly place to be. All the goodness is being killed off. And once God leaves, good luck.

"Confidence is not, 'They will like me.' Confidence is, 'I'll be fine if they don't.'" Unknown

PARENTAL UNITS

How I love the judgments of those who have no children. It makes me giddy. For how incredibly hard a job it can be at times.

When times are very lean and you struggle to provide. When health has failed and you still have to function.

When distance is between you, and only you, attempt to fill that gap.

It is one of the most difficult jobs you will ever do. And it is done, by most, with a great love and devotion.

It is a job that offers no health coverage. No annual salary. No year end bonuses. Guarantees extra work during all holidays. Plenty of overtime. No sick days. And generally a lonely life when retirement finally kicks in accompanied by empty-nest syndrome.

So if you make it through the many long years of childhood to adulthood, and do so with more than one child. Well, I call that success.

If you blessed enough to have your children grow into wonderful young adults, respectful, hardworking, intelligent, self-reliant. It means you have done something right. Your hard efforts have paid off.

For those who have never had the experience of carrying each child to term, literally growing human beings inside of you. And all the complications and discomfort that brings. All the childhood illnesses, bad dreams, behavior issues, education, doctors, dentists, vacations, movies, games, entertainment, exercise, employment, driving, dating, etc., etc.

Parents take many a back seat to their children to ensure they always have what they need and want. Parents who *don't* abuse their children. Parents who do without so their children can do with.

So, if you have never had a child, I really don't feel you have anything to stand on when it comes to judging others who *have* marched down that road.

Some children are truly grateful to their parents. Some merely throw crumbs when it suits them. And they literally believe that's enough after all that has been done for them. Think about it. With three children I was pregnant for twenty-seven months. Two years and three months. And I had three children in a four-year period. Not only is that hard on the body, it's terribly hard on a mother's emotional state. Parenthood can drain you. Especially, if you're not fortunate enough to have any family to help. Being all alone to do the job 24/7 is rough. But your kids don't see that. And if you do your job well, that's a good thing.

It's a touch business raising kids to adults. You never know how it will turn out, and sometimes, nothing like you thought it would ever be.

Life is messy. Shit happens. And we are *not* in control. For all we endure in our lives, and our efforts, against many odds. To raise human beings, plus provide for them, as well as, for ourselves. Please don't judge another person's journey until you have booked passage and traveled it for yourself.

Otherwise, it's just white noise to me.

"If you have been brutally broken, but *still* have the courage to be gentle to others, then you deserve a love deeper than the ocean itself."

Nikita Gill

MONSTERS

Her little feet could only go so fast. She ran through the back kitchen door, past the fireplace in the living room, and up the flight of stairs. Not even looking back to see how close her mother was to reaching out and grabbing her.

As she ran through the Dutch door at the top of the stairs, she slammed the bottom shut and headed for the bedroom she shared with her sisters. She heard the door fly open with such a force it literally shook the entire house.

Panic devoured her as she tried to catch her breath. Her heart was beating so hard, she felt it would explode inside of her chest. She held on as tightly as she could to the iron frame of the bare bed.

Her mother stormed in with that look. The look that she has seen countless times before. The look that meant nothing good was about to happen. That look that made her shake out of control.

Her mother began to yank, and pull, on her little arms. But she refused to go without a fight. Her mother was prying her hands off the iron rail. Pulling her fingers back. But the little one held tight. Her mother began slapping her face. And when *that* didn't work, she began punching her.

With such a beating the little one could hold on no longer, and was snatched by her hair, which her mother wrapped tightly around her hand. She was dragged by her hair. The little one held on to her head because the pain was so unbearable.

Her mother headed for the small built in crawl space that was in the little girl's bedroom. The little one knew what was coming and fought even harder!

Her mother held tight to the hair wrapped around one hand as she opened the locked small door with the other. As soon as the door was opened her mother picked the little girl up and threw her inside.

The floor of the crawl space was only wood beams with sheet beneath them. And the low ceiling had beams and thick pink insulation stuffed in between.

The little one fell with such force her knees were scraped and began to bleed. And then, the little door to the crawl space slammed shut and was locked from the outside. She fumbled in the pitch black crawl space she had found herself locked in so many time before.

She began to scream and cry. Banging on the little door *begging* her mother to please open the door. The crawl space ran along the entire second floor of the house, and only had two small doors. One in each bedroom that was upstairs.

The little girl tried to crawl, as fast as she could, along the unfinished floor in an attempt to reach the other door *before* her mother did. As she crawled in the pitch black, weeping and sweating from the extreme heat and panic. She could hear her mother, as well, running to that second door!

The little one crawled on broken pieces of very old glass Christmas ornaments. She could feel her flesh being cut open but was so obsessed with trying to reach that other door that she was numb to it.

As she got within *inches* of the door she heard her mother on the other side locking it. Her mother screamed, "You'll never get out now!!"

The little one started to hyperventilate. She was so frightened and just screamed and screamed. Begging her mother to let her out.

"Please mommy!!! Please let me out!! I can't breathe!!"

But her screams fell to the ground. She listened with her ear against that door, as her mother walked away, went through the Dutch door and slammed it behind her.

The little one wept until she could weep no more. The heat was unbearable but the small space and blackness was worse. She could see nothing. She was afraid of spiders coming to get her. Afraid of never being let out.

The heat and no air began to take its toll on her small body. She started to vomit. Her head felt as if it was going to explode. It hurt so bad. Then she felt her nose begin to bleed.

She banged on the small locked door until her knuckles were raw. Freaking out, kicking the door, and trying anything to break it down.

She remained locked in that dark, sweltering hole all day long. By the time her mother unlocked the door it was already dark outside. And when she unlocked it, she found the little one laying in her own vomit and urine.

Her mother just looked at her daughter and told her what a disgusting pig she was. That she smelled and now needed a bath. The little one knew what that meant. But she was so utterly exhausted, so thirsty, that she had no fight left in her.

She marched silently, obediently to the only bathroom located downstairs and stood watching, in a daze, as her mother filled the tub with scalding hot water. She then climbed in, when ordered, and her mother proceeded to scrub her soft flesh raw with cleanser.

There were no tears left to cry. There was no fight left. For this little on ad been broken so often she had lost count. This was her existence. The routine of living under the roof with a sociopath as a mother.

No dinner for such bad little girls. She was sent back upstairs after her brutal bath time. To a barren bed that waited for her. She laid on her back and stared at the dark ceiling over her. As she drifted off to sleep, the nightmares kicked in. So frightened by them, that she woke up in a urine soaked bed.

She had been beaten into submission. She had been scrubbed into silence. And this was a *good* day for her. There were many worse days waiting for her.

There was no rescue planned for her. There was no empty days or nights for they were all filled with great pain and suffering.

No punishment was too hard for her. No limit was ever set. There was never a line her mother wouldn't cross. Most times her mother would be in such a violent frenzy that she wouldn't stop until she saw blood.

The little girl was grateful when she wasn't tied to the old metal iron frame of her bed. Each day was a day filled with her attempts to navigate walking on egg shells around her mother. Hoping she wouldn't do anything wrong to invoke the wrath of her mother.

How she tried so desperately to get her own mother to actually love her. She thought if only she could just get her to love her, that she might not hurt her.

How pathetic to want to earn the love of a monster who had abused her so horrifically!

There are many wounds that heal on our flesh with time and care. And then there are wounds that nobody can see but that *never* truly heal completely.

And it is those wounds that dwell within our very souls. The ones we search daily to find a cure for.

If you were fortunate enough to have had a mother who actually loved you, treated you with kindness. Brought you joy. Fall to your knees and thank God in Heaven. Because there are many who envy you for that gift.

"That moment when you can actually *feel* the pain in your chest from seeing or hearing that something that *breaks* your heart." Unknown

A WARD OF THE STATE

In memory of Sharon Kolaniak

When I was informed, by my step father, that my mother was in the hospital dying, I was told she had pneumonia.

She lasted maybe three days or so, not really sure. My brother called me to tell me she had died. My absolute first thought was, "My God I'm free!! I am finally free!! I am finally *safe*!!" And I wept for four days.

My baby brother Adam called me. He told me how he had the opportunity to see our mother while she was hooked up to tubes and in an apparent coma.

He told me how he bent over and whispered in her ear that he hoped, and prayed, she would "rot in Hell" and "suffer ten times worse what she had put us through." As well as, how much he "hated her!"

Then he told me that our mother did not die of pneumonia. That she had actually committed suicide.

I felt bad for my baby brother to be able to face her, on her death bed, and say what he had said to her. I'm not sure I would have had the courage to.

Her suicide opened a whole new chapter in my life.

I had not laid eyes on my mother in *years*. But I had been permitted to see my sister Sharon through these years. Sharon was always allowed to come and stay with me and my husband. My mother would allow me to send plane tickets, with a chaperone inclusion, to fly Sharon cross country to stay with me.

Even though Sharon was three years older than me, she was my baby sister. Sharon was born with Downs Syndrome, and her mental age was about that of a seven or eight year old.

Sharon loved Barbie dolls and crayons for her coloring books. Being with my mother she had allowed *her* to collect the monies left to Sharon when our father blew his brains out. As well as, collecting her own Social Security.

But after my mother died I knew, no matter what, there was no way in Hell I was leaving my sister Sharon.

So I devised a plan that I made with my brother Teddy, who also lived in California at the time. A few weeks after they had buried my mother, and no, I did *not* attend her funeral. But I had learned a few things while living under their damn roof.

Connie, my mother, *never* worked. She survived off the monies she robbed from her kids jobs *and* off of my sister Sharon's benefits received monthly.

So I flew out to California with a two way ticket for Sharon. I flew out alone and was to turn around and leave the very next day with my sister Sharon.

Now, if you *think* returning to my mother's home was an easy thing to do after so many years, you would be quite mistaken. Even as I share this, I feel like someone is choking me and my heart is beating out of my chest.

Sharon pick me up at LAX. It took a couple of hours, because of the damn traffic, to get back to their place. I did get chance to see Teddy and his family. I did not know then that it would be the last time I would feel my brother's bear hug. He held me so tightly.

When we arrived at Connie's place, it was exactly as it had been so many years ago. I felt as if I would have a full blown panic attack! You truly have no idea what it took, and the faith that got me through that damn front door!

Sharon offered her room for me to sleep in, but there would be no sleep for me.

When she went to bed I waited a couple of hours before I got up and started looking around. I came across about a dozen big ole hat boxes. I began to open them up, one by one, and saw they were filled to the brim with photographs.

Each box was the same. I sat down on the floor and spent the next four hours looking through every single box. As each box was emptied and another begun, I started looking with more frenzy. I began to cry. I frantically looked at every single picture. Sometimes, in the same box, more than once!

I could not find *one* picture of me. Not one!

It was as if she had completely erased me out of existence. This made me feel sick and I ran to the bathroom to vomit.

I sat in a corner in the dining room, in the dark, weeping until the sun shown in its first light. I picked myself up and went to Sharon's bedroom to pack a bag for her.

When I heard Sharon was awake, I went to get her ready for the trip ahead. Suddenly, there was Sharon coming out of Connie's bedroom. I kept my cool, although I have no idea how.

Finally, we left for LAX. The traffic was phenomenal! I was panicking thinking we just weren't going to make our flight. We finally arrived and we waited for boarding.

My mind was pretty screwed up at this point. I was afraid that I was not going to make it on that damn plane with my sister. My heart was beating so hard and fast. I had to make several trips to the ladies room because I kept throwing up. I had not eaten anything, nor had a drink, since I had left Newark Airport in New Jersey.

Finally, we were able to board the plane. At this point, I was literally shaking like a leaf. Still afraid that Sharon might not be able to come with me.

We found our seats, I buckled Sharon's belt and we sat waiting for that damn plane to take off. We started moving. I was holding my sister's hand so tightly. We proceeded down the long runway. Waiting in line behind several other airplanes for take-off.

Our plane began its fast run and within minutes we were airborne! I can no longer hold it together. I break down in tears. My sister sees me crying and says, "It's okay, Diane. It's okay now." Her words just made me cry more. My sweet angel Sharon.

We landed in New Jersey and I have her safe with me. Within literally hours of landing, I race to the local Social Security office in Brick, with my sister. I inform them to immediately to stop sending her checks to Connie's address.

I also informed them that I didn't want them either. That I was quite capable of taking care of my sister. For first time in my sister's life, she was not wanted for her damn money.

I had no idea what this action was going to unleash. And how it was literally going to change our lives forever.

As you can imagine, it did not go over well. I called my brother Teddy. Suddenly, my own brother was yelling at me. Telling me I had no right in stopping Sharon's *money*! And that it would be best to, "send her back to California."

I was floored! I had stood in my brother's kitchen just days earlier and we had both *agreed* on my course of action. It was very well planned out. I was livid!!

Days passed having many conversations with my brother Teddy. It was finally agreed that I would send Sharon back to California. And this would ensure I wouldn't be arrested. Which at the time, I had no idea that since my sister Sharon was over the age of 18, *she* could decide where she wanted to live. This late obtained information shall haunt me till the day I die.

My brother Teddy said he would take Sharon in. Not sure what the difference was between her staying with me, or staying with him. At least with me, she would not have been abused and used just for her damn money! I tried to report Connie for neglect when I saw the state my sister's teeth were in. But the Social Security Office really didn't know what to do, so they said.

With a broken heart, and spirit, I sat in Newark Airport waiting for Sharon to board yet another plane. I sat there holding her hand. Trying desperately not to cry. But when the time came for our final hug, I wept. I can still hear Sharon saying, "Don't cry Diane. It's okay."

She went to live with Teddy as planned. I was grateful she would never go back to Connie's again. I had, at the very least, accomplished that much.

But there was yet another damn chapter of hell I would be forced to deal with.

A story to continue tomorrow.

"Three things cannot be long hidden,
the sun, the moon, the truth."

Confucius

"Adulthood is like looking both way before you cross the
street, and then getting hit by an airplane." Unknown

OPEN WOUND

Flesh of my flesh, your betrayal was swift and deep.

The scar shall remain open and unhealed. Summer heat cannot bring new life. Winter's cold will embrace the death.

I have allowed you to devour me. I have been swallowed by attentiveness to your every whim.

To break free, in your mind, you had to break all others in your heart. A pain you have inflicted, which shall endure the test of time.

Flesh of my flesh, you have peeled the skin from my very soul. You have chosen to forget who has given you your first breath.

You have forgotten the first sight you beheld. And taken the first words of great love to the bottom of your memory.

You have slain the very heart you grew from.

Tears drawn from such a deep place in my soul that are mixed with blood.

A stone that has grown inside of me. A stone that weighs me down. A stone I cannot seem to remove. A stone that has replaced the encompassing love that was brought to me through your existence.

You have robbed me of the gift God had chosen to bestow upon my wretched flesh.

You had no right to.

The suffering you have drowned me in shall revisit you. The pain you have delivered shall be gathered unto you.

Will *you* survive all you have rendered? Or will you break under the weight of such absolute agony?

For no one escapes the fate of sorrow given to one whom is undeserving. It shall return to thee, even if I am buried. It shall return to thee.

"You only life once, but if you do it right, once is enough."

Mae West

STILLNESS

It's the silence that gets to me the most.

There's no random talking. No laughter. No arguing.

There's no dishes or pans clanking in the background. No washer or dryer running continuously.

There's no doors opening and shutting. No footsteps climbing the stairs.

There's no blaring TV's you need to demand lowering of. There's not even any sneezing that needs blessing.

No more sharing how days have gone. No more sharing what bills need attention. No more master list posted on the fridge door of groceries needed.

No need to announce, "I'm home!" when walking through the front door.

No need for big planned meals when a simple bowl of cereal will suffice for one. A loaf of bread goes bad before it's even finished.

The silence is deafening. The loneliness is over whelming.

In my heart this isn't the way it is supposed to be. As parents we take care and give our children every spare moment. All our attention. Love and kindness, and sacrifice our world to ensure their world is a good one.

Reminds me of my faith. We cannot gain entrance, or access, to heavenly Father by our *works*, so that none may boast.

It's the same with being a parent. You work 24/7 for decades, and in the end, you certainly don't gain access to anything just because of all our efforts.

So the care givers are left behind. Some have told me the process is the same as mourning a death. Try mourning three.

So we step back and stay out of the way. We bury our despair so far down into our soul. We grieve silently, just as the silence surrounds us.

The adjustment has not been an easy one. A lot of depression. The best part of the day now is to sleep. Because when I sleep, I don't have to feel.

I stay in a constant siege of prayer. Afraid the fragility will break me in two.

I really have no desire to be in this place I find myself. And I am trying desperately to dig myself out. Very hard when I feel the hole is bottomless.

May Father continue to bless me and keep me in His tender care.

"Everything is hard before it is easy." Goethe

ONE YEAR

There are always certain memories that stand out the most for each of us. Ones that have taught us so much. Ones we never felt we were quite worthy enough for.

There was such a time when fear was not my enemy. Because there was no fear.

Someone who taught me many things. Things I never knew of. Philosophy, psychology, and most important, exploration.

Climbing upon ancient rock ruins and crawling between mountains squeezed together. Sitting on the very edge of cliffs while eagles ride the winds before you.

Sliding down slopes of cold water climbing over smooth rocks. And paddling in a canoe to a small island for an afternoon picnic.

It was freedom to me.

Climbing stairs to the rooftop of Mohonk Mountain House. Gazing into the beautiful endless summer sky as a full moon hung throwing off it's light.

Scaling rock sides to extreme heights to be able to stand on the top of the world.

Sleeping under a blanket of stars beneath the fragrant scent of apple trees. The smell was intoxicating.

Being taught how to cross country ski. Only to retreat in front of a roaring fire while sipping hot cocoa. Watching as the snow fell for hours.

So much beauty to be a part of. So many amazing days and nights seeing life through another's eyes.

I had no fear. There was no pain. No demons to ruin, what seemed, our beautiful journey.

The grave mistake comes when we, somehow, believe we are not worthy of such. So we push it away.

We make decisions that influence the rest of our lives.

But we can never go back.

I was so different. I had dreams that I believe could be fulfilled. I had chased the nightmares away.

But the past wasn't done with me. And it was more powerful than any Category 5 hurricane.

I have no regrets. I may have disappointments. Broken heart. Bitterness and great sorrow, but not for things I have done or experienced.

At times, I feel I have experienced far too much. Too much loss. Too much anger. Too much sorrow. And I try to even my thought process out.

I have experienced many blessings. Too many to keep track of. I have shared much love. I have beautiful children. I was told I would never have children and tried for twelve years. Then was blessed with, not one, but three.

I have a home, a forever home. Something I have never had before.

My cup truly runneth over.

My faith is my ultimate sustainer. I pray without ceasing. How I pray love would infect the entire planet, as easily as, evil has.

When we all look back as our years gather, there are some who stand out in our memories. Some whom we have loved with our entire hearts. Some we will never forget. Some who showed us a world we never knew before them. And have not been able to recapture since then.

I wonder, "Where has the person I *used* to be with them gone?"

"Be strong enough to stand alone. Smart enough to know when you need help. And brave enough to ask for it." Unknown

NEST

How sad when the last chick flies. The nest becomes empty and is no longer needed.

In a short time, all the small twigs and leaf insulation dries up and is carried away on the gentle breezes of summer.

Looking back on all the events and occasions which led up to this very moment. Time was cruel to advance so quickly.

Fluffy down feathers grew real wings, able to support flight.

As mom and dad watch as their last little chick flies away, never once looking back, they wonder if it was all worth it after all.

Those chicks who have occupied so much of their time. Such great devotion, care and love. Was it worth it knowing the day would surely come when those chicks would no longer need them?

How hard to be so invested in the smallest of creatures. So dependent upon the care and love of parents that, without such care, they would have literally died.

Now to be back where you started, two birds alone in a nest. The sounds of the endless chirping taken away. The endless feeding and grooming gone forever.

How hard it was to adjust to having new chicks to tend and raise. A complete life change. Readjusting every single aspect of life.

Only to be replaced with silence.

What an emptiness that is left behind. A sadness. But those little chicks who have captured flight and left the nest, will one day understand what it feels like. Just like their mom and dad do.

Some birds dream of having a huge family. But never see it. And some birds dream of having no family but are surrounded by many.

This old momma bird misses all her chicks and cherished every single moment, and memory, because she *knew* one day her chicks would take

flight. Each one taking a piece of her with them.

Love your baby chicks while you can. Before you know it you'll turn around and find an empty nest blowing away in the wind of a summer's breeze.

"Where there is no struggle, there is no strength." Unknown

SOJOURNERS

When I needed personal care during many illnesses, You were my only physician.

When I was broken and filled with utter despair, You were my only friend.

When I had no peace of mind, You comforted me.

I can't imagine surviving *one day*, or one long night, without You by my side.

Your Word is engraved upon my very soul. Your light guides me in my darkness. Your truth settles all doubts. Your mercy covers me.

My desire is to walk with God. To hear His voice and gaze upon His face.

How wonderful a day that will be. We are merely sojourners. Temporary visitors here. Just passing thru on our way back home. So keep those spiritual bags packed my friends!

"A meaningful silence is always better than meaningless words." Unknown

SILENCE

God goes silent on us all.

If you happen to understand that statement, you have been where many live.

Only problem I have with it, is why. Why does He go silent on us?

I have come to realize that it is *not* always a test of *faith*, but a test of *strength*. Yes, His grace may be sufficient, but sometimes in our deepest hour of struggle, His touch is what's desired most.

"We all die. The goal isn't to live forever. The goal is to create something that will live forever." Unknown

SOMEONE

Someone died today. Someone was born today.

Someone was diagnosed with stage 4 cancer today. Someone went into remission.

Someone's home burned to the ground today. Someone just moved into their first home.

Someone was beaten today by another's fist. Someone was held close and told they were loved.

Someone went to bed feeling the sides of their stomach touching from hunger. Someone threw out their dinner because they were full.

Someone went to bed cold and shivering from no heat. Someone is walking around barefoot because there's heat in their floors.

Someone was wrongfully terminated today. Someone else was just hired in their dream job.

Someone is utterly alone today. Someone else is surrounded by friends and family.

Someone has given up on life and God today. Someone else is holding fast to their faith in God's mercy.

Diane M. Reaves

We all carry a cross.

We all have a story.

But if we decide that we will be there for others, and think less of ourselves, we will make the world a far better place.

Someone is dreaming today. Someone else is living in reality.

"People will *never* forget how you made them *feel*." Maya Angelo

LIES

Everything I thought I knew was just a lie.

I believed good things happen to good people – lie.

Justice is gotten by all who have been treated unjustly – lie.

If you give your life to your children, you will be a blessed woman – lie.

Family will always be there for you, especially, when you need them the most – lie.

Being faithful means that faithfulness will come back to you – lie.

All prayers are answered – lie.

What you do to others is done to you – lie.

Liars will always be found out and the truth shall set you free – lie.

If you work very hard at your job, you will be rewarded and appreciated – lie.

If you show true love to those who hate you, eventually, they will grow to love you – lie.

We each get what we deserve – lie.

True love last forever – lie.

Time heals all wounds – lie.

Life is full of ironies. Life is full of disappointments. Life is hard as hell. Life is littered with liars and deceivers who lack any sense of remorse.

If you are lucky enough to have had a great childhood. Lucky enough to have a great family, and extended family. Lucky enough to have children who truly care about you. Lucky enough to have a great career. Lucky enough to have real friends, then you are *not* among the majority.

For most of us know exactly how screwed up life really is. How rare the glimpses of joy are. And how much we long to be in a far better place where none of this life, and what it does to people, will even matter.

"We are all a little broken. But the last time I checked, broken crayons still color the same." Unknown

INCLINETHYEARTOMYVOICE

I cried out to God till I had no voice. No answer came.

To feel *that* alone.
To loose all hope.
To be alive in a living Hell.

That kind of pain and darkness lingers. It moves ever so slowly. Every minute of suffering being forever carved into memory.

You mind cannot fathom the very hands that bring you such suffering, are the same hands you were born from.

You imagine, "If I can just get her to *see* me. To see the pain she is causing me. Maybe then something will snap. Change inside of her."

But she looks into my eyes. Piercing into my soul. She *sees* my fear. She *sees* my pain. She *hears* my cries. But there is nothing that *I* see in *her* eyes.

There is only darkness.
There is no love.
There is no mercy.
There is no compassion.

There is only death.

There are still nightmares that creep into my dreams. There are still times I wake up and find myself gasping for air.

There are still morning when I am woken by my own uncontrollable weeping. Times when I have to convince myself *all over again* that I am **safe.**

OLD SOUL

I am an old soul.
My flesh has seen better days.
My mind has endured far too many mental battles.
But I have lived.
I have traveled to many parts of our world.
I have watched as people have fought over dirt and stone.
And watched as some have tried to conquer a people's very soul.
I have given birth. And know the feeling of seeing a first breath.
Hearing a first sound made.
I have also killed.
I know the pain of regret and eternal sorrow.
I am victorious in surviving many harsh storms blown across my flesh
and battles for my soul.
I know what it feels likes to be filled with sin and live in darkness.
I know what it feels like to be forgiven and to forgive.
I know what it is like to recognize the connection of my soul to a
Creator who has not yet given up on me.
I know what it is like to weep for my own pain.
But I also know what it is like to weep for another's pain.
What can I teach a young one?
What wisdom could a warrior of this life share to ease another's
battle?
Why would my words have any more weight than your words?
I *know* the price Another has paid for my soul.

I know Another has endured great pain and suffering for the likes of me.

I know my soul had to be purchased by a Sacrifice I was not even worthy to make.

And this was done *before* I existed.

I know there is nothing, ever, that I could do to obtain this grace; this eternal salvation.

No amount of works. Even if I spent my entire life trying, I would fall miserably short.

Who among us would volunteer to *die* in order to save *countless* souls?

Who among us would volunteer to have flesh torn from our bones at the end of a spiked whip?

Who among us would volunteer to be spit upon and have thorns dug deep into our skull?

Who among us would volunteer to have nails driven into both our hands and our feet?

If we lived to be 400 years old, we could *never* come close to repaying such a debt!

How does One die for others He has never met? Let alone millions and millions?

Each of us walk a different road. No two roads are the same.

You do not know my agony. I do not know yours.

As in any war, some have far more scars than others.

As in war, some are changed forever by it.

You cannot walk thru a fire and not be burned.

My soul is an old warrior.

My soul knows love.

My soul understands compassion and empathy.

My soul will live for eternity.

Perhaps joining other souls when I leave this place. Perhaps visiting endless other worlds.

If our Creator, "*knew* us before we were in our mother's womb," who was I then?

Did I have time to prepare for the journey I was to take?
Did I know all I would be forced to endure?
Did our Creator know?
Does He already know which of us will return unto Him and which will decide to be an eternal enemy?

How many of us will bring others to our eternal fate with us? Or will they be bringing us?
I have known heroes in my life. Unspoken heroes who probably have no idea the impact they had in my journey.
I have also known villains and dark demons who have attempted to destroy me.
Oh, if we could see the many angels and warriors that surround us!
To reach out and touch them. Knowing they *are* there.
How do you teach another how to survive?
How to endure the worse kind of pain in their entire life?
You cannot.
Some will not be able to endure and decide to give up.
Some will be taken from us.
And the rest of us will soldier on.
Lingering between here and what is to come.
Breathing out of habit and *not* out of choice.
Counting the hours which turn into years.
Always waiting. Always expecting.
Knowing when the moment finally does arrive, we *shall* recognize His voice. And we shall joyfully return where we started.

Live in love.
Bury others in mercy.
Offer your heart to those in agony.
Humble yourself before all.
Teach patience.

And never for a single moment forget who it is that resides in your heart.

The End

Printed in the United States
By Bookmasters